City Gray
Country Blue

Brett Blandford

PublishAmerica
Baltimore

© 2008 by Brett Blandford.
All rights reserved. No part of this book may be reproduced, stored in a retrieval system or transmitted in any form or by any means without the prior written permission of the publishers, except by a reviewer who may quote brief passages in a review to be printed in a newspaper, magazine or journal.

First printing

PublishAmerica has allowed this work to remain exactly as the author intended, verbatim, without editorial input.

ISBN: 1-60474-301-8
PUBLISHED BY PUBLISHAMERICA, LLLP
www.publishamerica.com
Baltimore

Printed in the United States of America

Thank you Dave
Budd Bil May 08'

In Regent Park

On lonely benches
business suits
keep brown-bag dates
a fifth of truth
getting stoned
growing old

With wandering eyes
old men watch
the pretty girls
in skinny skirts
soiled sighs
unspoiled thighs

Overhead
the El cars rush
urban thunder
past tired faces
stolid stares
mortared glares

In Regent Park
the lonely wait
the idle hours
like worn-out art
a gallery
of gorgon gray
shadows congregate
in Regent Park

where the faithful
come to pray

A Snowy Day

It's starting to snow.
He's asleep, I watch
the dirty sky.
To the west a
sliver of red,
to the east, the funnels
of River Rouge rise
above the endless
rows of houses,
downtown dirty.

"He's sleeping peacefully,"
her unfamiliar accent awakened me.
How ironic, a black woman,
prejudice soiled his life
now the last to care,
a black woman.

Dirty downtown black,
ride the bus black,
tuna salad for lunch,
always on a diet black.
Church on Sunday,
work on Monday black.
She stared in compassion
I stared in stereotype.

He's sleeping, the snow has stopped.
Watching him, I'm reminded
of the time he asked me
to go fishing,
he never asked me before.
I know he liked it
I didn't go

I should have.

I remember his stories
the runnin' rum and sharkin',
of prohibition
and of the hammer shop.

Hot iron, heavy forged
his life, hot, loud, strong always hoping we'd find a better life.

Only I found the heat of the press
and the knowledge of the iron,
it is good knowledge.

He is sleeping, the snow has stopped.
I touch his sleeping hand
his eyes awaken,
though not the expression I know.
But the stare of the embalming fluid,
pain killers pumped into his sleep.

I hope he didn't see me

I was walking away,

and the snow was starting to fall

Without Words

Without words
I am not the one
who speaks in endless diaphragms
of whisper willing silk
draped across your trembling flesh
becoming lost in tangled amber waves.
Whose touch suppressed an anxious breath
as heartbeats rose on ebbing tides
as strawberry metaphors laughed upon
your naked flesh and wind 'round limbs
to cinch a breath

Without words,
a moonless night
no silvern light, my caress lost
in empty solemn shadow
without words…
without you

Let Fall the Night

Let fall the night
the breath of twilight's mist
two lovers lay
b'neath the sighing moon
across the sky
phantoms playing indigo blue
subtle breaths
laughter of a fragrant air
the coming storm
whispers, through her hair.
Let fall the night
to satin lavender pleas
and taste the flesh of ev'ning

To Die in Your Arms

To die in your arms
to lay amid the fragrance of your flower
rapt in the veil of your embrace
Still, my head held
within your tearful gaze
the taste of saline crystals
falls upon my lips
Your heartbeat oh, but a whisper
draped in silken cinnamon waves
Life through amber plays
ebbing on unending tides
To look upon the silver sequined
horizon
that is your eyes

Sunday Afternoon

The snow is falling
light and soft,
tumbling whispers
that land on eyelashes
and playful tongues
dancing on an angel's breath breeze
that blushes cheeks
and tickles noses.
arms in arms keeping warm
keeping close
gloves in pockets
boots on pavement
dimestore windows
dressed in holiday cheer
beneath a gray
woolen blanket sky

Autumn Gray

The sky is autumn
October gray
faded, lifeless
like lunch bag leaves that swirl
as dervish fiends
across empty parking lots
in corners
of buildings cold and gray
my heels upon the concrete
echo up the empty faces
echo'd steps, empty faces
lifeless sky
on the wind a drizzle
faints the distant scenes
dampness to mark my steps
it is cold
the sky is gray
I am alone

A Rainy October Day

The rain is falling
not a hard rain
but rain just the same
relentless in its passion
to fill ponds and sidewalks
it continues undisturbed
by nature or by man

The rain is falling
a steady rain that
spatters the windows creating
tiny giggling rivers that trickle down the glass
each bearing their own course
only to vanish into the
wind weathered cracks of the old sills

The rain is falling
not a cold rain
but cold enough to chill the air
and blanket the garden green
with a crystal glistened dew
that rivals the dead gray pitch
of the cotton October sky

The rain is falling
not just any rain
but a rain that gambols along
rooftops and cobblestone
while I in my failings
can just sit in awe
of the concert on display

The Prisoner

I've seen you from my window
you pass by every day
your quiet steady pace
goes unseen by all but me.
And as you pass on by like
the Eleanor Rigbys of this world
you wear your loneliness like
a coat against the cold.
Embracing the only one that you can trust

I see you from my window
you pass by every day
the bitter frost that burns so deep
clings to your every breath.
And as the world goes on
and you keep your shackled course
mourning every step along the way
I'll see you from my window
you'll pass by every day

The Old Book

Surprisingly
the ink remains as
calculated Indian stains
that still emit an acrid
odour of the presses
oiled block.

An arrow marks the
spot where some other
lonely adventurer trod
long ago before the
leather and bond
evinced of time
encrusted shelf

The Dance

Alone on a park bench on a cold winter's day
silently watching the snow
I pulled up my collar to fend off the cold
a tender voice whispered, hello
I turned, startled to see you standing there
I stood to meet your eyes with mine
Standing in wonder, as you reached out to me
I felt the warmth in your smile.
Suddenly somewhere a band started playing
an old but familiar tune

We laughed as we danced holding each other close
in the spotlight, a gift from the moon
And like Fred and Ginger on the silver screen
we danced 'neath a halo of stars
And as others around us stopped to applaud
we danced like the dance floor was ours.
Dancing and spinning to the music that played
we had both let our spirits soar.

Then the room became silent, and we were alone
you whispered that you had to go
I watched then in silence you fading away
til I found myself sitting alone
on a park bench, on a cold winter's day
silently watching the snow

Left in the Rain

Bouquet
of flowers,Caught
in the rain
standing here holding a dream

A kiss
and a promise
lost in the wind
blowing away on the breeze

Rivers
of memories, flow
gently by
meandering back to the sea

Hours
like shadows
waning away
never is life as it seems

Streetlights
like stagelights
Cast
garish tones
an actor alone on the stage

Bouquet of flowers
left in the rain

The Bus Is Late

Who is she, who stands
silently
in the pouring rain.
Like spring's first bloom
wither'd and quail
against winter's masquerade.
As raindrops
deftly dance
upon her china face
mascara stains her placid cheeks
once blushed, caressed, and kissed.
Blithe curls lay quietly
sullen
limp against the velvet suede
as whispered chills
run down her spine
her eyes remain transfixed
on garish headlights darting
over ink black puddled pools.

Still she waits…

(the bus is late)

Midnight Rain

Softly, gently
the quiet rain
that whispers,
upon the silent pane
wanders down
in tiny strands
to the waiting sill.
Ever changing.
Ever the same.
Silent, blind
with only the
distant strains
of cello to guide,
I breathe my fingers
through your hair.
Softly, gently

Have You Ever Heard

Have you ever heard
The sound of lightning
threading through a pastel charcoal sky
before obtrusive heavy footfalls
thunder across the plain.
The sound of a sleeping ocean
breathe upon the shore
til dawn's hurried brilliance
explodes along the strand.
The sound of slowly melting snow
into the forgiving forest loam
as an unsure weeping drizzle
chatters purple budding limbs
The laughter of a breeze.
The furrow of a kite.
A windmill turning aimlessly without a care.
Or the surrendering sigh, of the setting sun
into a cool,
satin sheet horizon.

The River

Beneath the halo'd cobalt moon

the river dreams

in quietude............still,

beneath her velvet veil

Bourbon Masquerade

She came upon the bourbon scene
in a dress she borrowed from Halloween,
stealing stares, an' whiskey promises,
from every sideburn an' tattoo
at the bar
With a wink of wry pretension
she wears a painted laugh, and finds
the bottom of the glass with clouded eyes.
Silk and satin, garter and lace
groping glares cling to hips,
and drip down thighs
like water on a glass.
Polished, perfumed, glistening
of wanton woman wine
in the violet neon spotlight
she prefers it on the rocks.
No winners, no losers, only jaded fragments
hidden deep beneath the shades
of evening hues

Shadows

The playful shadows
That danced the cobbled walks
Now hide in silence of the mourning gray
That brought the palling rain
Shadows cede to wrinkled stares
Of coarse walls and pillars
The gates, of black wrought iron
That spike and rise to touch a faceless sky

Across the way
In silence waits
The gilded mounts of yesterday
Circus reds and faded blue hues
As echoes of a bygone era
Swirl about the quiet carousel
That upon a time sent favoured tunes
Across the garden green

As the linger of roasted peanuts looms
On the ancient summer breeze
That teased a million multicoloured balloons
And giggled through the emerald bonnets
Of elm and oak
Canopies reflect the hues of a boding sky

Hunched against the rain
A silent figure through the mist
Unkept hair, matted at the ends,
Lays wet upon the shoulders
Of His ancient overcoat
He wanders silently
Lost among the shadows
Of his yesterdays

Whither

With bated breath
Intent alone
To hear her voice once more
His heart sinks with
Every tone
Ring – ring, ring – ring,
click

Silent Pose

In silent pose
Shadows meld with depth of light
Captured. Beheld
In a sliver of time
The incidence of light and dark
The mind's eye follows the
course of filtered light, only to be seduced
Into the complicities of shadows
Revealed in the intricacies
Of the pose

The Park Bench

Weathered and rusting
the wrought iron bench sits quiet
as wildgrass grows course
around its legs.
The seat and back are in need of paint
and the path is rough
with overgrowth.
Overhead, a large oak looms,
whose time twisted branches,
most bare of leaves.
shade out much of the sun
On occasion young lovers pass-by
but their voices are quiet,
whispers huddled
shoulder to shoulder in dark coats
against the afternoon gray
My ears are keen
to the quick tight step of high-heel boots,
hoping, maybe.

I often sit there, on that bench,
reading till the evening halo glows cold
'round the sulfur lamppost
and I know its time to leave.
The last bus will be by soon, but
tomorrow I will be back.

Perhaps one afternoon
I'll bring some paint
and paint that bench
pull a few weeds even.
Perhaps that tumbling page of newspaper
won't escape my chase
and I'll fold it into my pocket.
I can read it on the bus ride home.

Beneath the Ageless Sycamore

He shows up with the Sunday crowd,
and takes his seat beneath the ageless **sycamore**.
A leftover plaid jacket and tired baggy pants
floppy shoes and worn-out knees, he sits quietly.
A bag of peanuts in his hands.

With somber eyes and painted smile
as real as pastel drawings on the street,
as real as the comedic nose on his face.
He sits, his legs crossed at the knees
and watches the children play.

A scuffed-up worn out derby sits
cockeyed on his head.
Whisps of tangled white and gray
protrude haphazardly.

His thoughts, his own as he waits,
the children come to be entertained.
As adults regard this jackaled vagabond
with the daisy in his lapel,
since forever.
"He must be a drunk," they've come to say
as coloured silks reveal,
rubber balls that seem to vanish,
within time worn vaudeville tricks.

He plays silently, this curious old man,
to a jaundiced crowd
that grievously toss coins at his feet.
That when they're gone he slowly stoops, to retrieve.
Beneath the ageless sycamore.

Do You Still Know Me

Do you still know me,
Though not of melded shadow light
a filament of time
a whisper of breath
a passing glimpse to something
that turns your head, yet nothing

Do you still know me
Though not a raindrop upon your cheek
or caress of summer's playful breeze
through your hair
A daring snowflake
upon your eyelash

Do you still know me
Though not a voice, rather a breath
a phone call in the night
or the seductive fingertip splash
of a warm afternoon shower
~ shared ~

In the quiet of the night
Do you
~ Still ~.

Rhapsody in the Rain

I watch the raindrops
Fall against the frosted pane
Each one is you
I press my face and hands
To listen—your voice
Satin whispers
I turn the latch
And raise the sash
Your whispers fall upon my face
My body—warmed upon your touch
Fingertips—down chest
and shoulders chase,
Falling to my waist

Raindrops kiss—bliss
Upon trembling lips
Pausing in a moment
To taste each one
I pass my fingers
Through my hair
and bringing my lips to yours,

whisper your name
unto the night

Just Passing Through

I've passed this way so many times
these faces all the same
each one a silent reminder
watching, counting steps
with apathetic strains.
A traveler, wandering
like so many others
who have passed this way before,
hunched and wrought
against the angry storm.
We seek shelter for but a moment
in the embrace of soulful eyes.
Gray skies loom to beckon me,
through the mist
of melancholy song, I must be on my way.

For sadness is a long, lonely journey
and I have paused too long

One Moment of Silence

One moment of silence
We, who gave ask
Of little in return but,
One moment of silence

For it is in silence where
We dwell
We know not of your world
Nor you of ours
Yet for one moment,
We share the silence- a secret
Breeched only by the
Season's breath
Whispering through naked
November limbs
Beneath the still gray sky

One moment of silence
Passes slowly- each in your own thoughts
You search for meaning

It is ours
Our selflessness we share with you
In a breath of time In one moment of silence

Each Breath

With each breath;

Seconds become minutes
Become hours
On patent leather tides
with each breath;
Candle wax
descends slowly
Along, slender tapers
with each breath;
Evening breezes whisper
Teasing fingers
Unlacing midnight's satin veil
with each breath;
Surging energy- rising
To meet the need
Lightning sires the coming storm
with each breath

Excuse Me

Excuse me
Do I know you
Haven't we met somewhere before

Excuse me
Not to be rude
You look like someone I once knew

No, I've never worked there
No, I didn't go to that school
I don't think I know them
But then again…
I'm terrible with names

Excuse me
Don't you remember
Was it that cold December day
The Sunday in the park
Or the night we weathered that storm
And laughed against the dark

(if only you knew)
as you stepped through that door
that you were someone
I once knew

Listen

Listen
to the whispered hush of
the gently falling snow
as it slumbers down
on the tranquil forest
of lifeless limbs that reach
up thru the gray misted
voids of darkness

listen to the siren teasing
of the reckless wind as
it plays among the elm and birch
calling, only to run away
whipping winters' icy down
against my face
as your hoofs crunch
through the snow

A Thousand Miles Away

My love for you is ever clear
across the windswept darkened plain
though' distance blinds me yet from you
I ride on through the pouring rain
I can taste your tender wine sweet lips
in the rain streaking down my face
yet it can't wash away the bitter tears
or miles left standing in the way
I know you're waiting on the horizon
I hear your voice whispering on the wind
the thunder echoes out my anguished pain
of when I'll next be with you again

These callous hardened hands of leather
pull you close about your slender waist
my fingers glide along your shivering spine
as I tighten my grip upon the reins
My charger be both strong and brave
I curse its demon hearted soul
though' it could be, no more, for me
if it were yet two hundred fold

I can feel the whispered velvet softness
of your hair so cinder silken fine
as I draw you gently ever closer
to bring your trembling lips to mine
I just need to hold you in my arms
and let us to our music softly sway
though it seems I've rode an eternity
You're still a thousand miles away

Night Rider

On a southbound outta Tulsa
sleep was on my mind
nothin 'head but darkness
and nothin left behind
As the red eye's lonesome whistle
whispered passed the lights
I could feel a haunting presence
as I stared out through the night
Like a raven in the moonlight
he rode along the rise
and I watched him chase the shadows
across the desert sky
The car got winter quiet
an eerie chill fell on the air
that's when I heard a tired voice
that I never knew was there

His face was dark and weathered
whiskey on his breath
His eyes were ablaze with a devil's fire
and his tone was cold as death
He wore a hat and boots, a funeral suit
on his chest a silver pin
and he spun a mournful story
of the one who rides the wind
Some say he was a lawman
some say he killed a man
and now his tortured spirit
roams the backroads of this land
beneath the indigo of midnight
as his story did unfold

I sat in disbelief
at the tale that he told
He told me of a legend
of a woman, and a sin
the only one who knew the truth
behind the one who rides the wind

When the train pulled to the station
"end of the line," the captain cried
I stepped out on the platform the stranger, I could not find
So as the wind whipped up, I wondered
was all this on my mind...
Was I only dreamin
of the stranger, the woman, and the sin
of the lonely midnight phantom
riding on the wind

Cowboys Never Ride Alone

Cowboys never ride alone
As legend would dictate.
They've always had a partner
One they can relate.

You never really love him and
You never really know him
For his reasons are his own.
Yet he's one you can rely on
And he never rides alone

No cowboys never ride alone
Wherever they might roam.
For angels ride with cowboys
To show them the way home

So if you see a cowboy
And he seems far from home.
He's just living the life he loves
And he never rides alone..

On the Outskirts of Old San Antoine

In a lonely old barroom on the outskirts of old San Antoine
They asked if I had one more…before I would go
I told them I knew a pillow talk from a long time ago
So I started strummin some notes long, soft and slow

The barroom got quiet as the forgotten notes started to flow
About long auburn hair and eyes of Virginia coal
A smile that could melt a man, no matter how cold
The winter winds blow,
One night in her arms, I knew I could never let go

She had the voice of a Spanish guitar, melting the night
She spoke in a whisper, of warm Candle-light,
That night we shared firelight, and sipped sweet desert wine
Trembling in her touch, as our bodies entwined
My mind started chasing a vision of leather and lace
as the voice of the flat-top revealed the heartbreaking tale

A song of a Lady and a love that cannot be denied
A love song remembered, forgot over miles and time
A love I had lost long ago, come back in song
In a lonely old barroom on the outskirts of old San Antoine

The Legend of Ray McCabe

Six riders on a mission
a posse all their own
dark riders on journey
to bring a cowboy home

Riding through the darkness
to beat the break of day
six ride across the desert
to bring home Ray McCabe

Frank Casey was a lawman
who met Ray in a bar
Ray had shown a faster gun
Frank's forehead bears the scar

William was a hero
the strong and handsome type
called Ray out in Dallas
and quickly lost his life

Johnny was a greenhorn
whose luck ran out one day
he rode into Laredo
and just got in the way

Bill and Pete were brothers
who worked the Diamond T
Ray had caught them napping
and shot them in their sleep

From Texas came a ranger
to meet Ray on his own
He rode in on an Arab
in a box, they sent him home

Chance came along, a drifter
thought to be Ray's best
Ray met him in an alley
and put a bullet through his chest

They met up with him in Texas
In a forgotten border town
long since been deserted
the buildings crumbling down
They stopped outside a hotel
the posse knew the place
they called out the gunfighter
to meet them face to face

I recognize your faces
why do you haunt me now
but I'll come out you cowards
and again I'll gun you down

He met them in the alley
and not a rider moved
they rode out for the gunman
that he might know the truth

They showed him in the shadows
a dismal lonely grave
a weather beaten marker
bore the gunman's name

He begged the spectral riders
No, this can't be true
they said the army caught you
in 1852

Seven spectral riders
riders of the purple sage
rode out of time forgotten
to bring home Ray McCabe

Changes

So you're making some changes...Me? still the same
Here, I bought these for you...sure looks like rain
He says he doesn't love you, but you're still holding tight
to promises he'll never keep...No, just something in my eye
Out here, winters can be so cold...the sky sure looks like snow
You say how much you're missing him...why don't you just go.

Pretty blue-jean lady, so tender yet so strong
A lonely, haunting whistle sings an empty song
That whistle's lonely echo stealing 'cross the plain
Sends a broken-hearted signal...that
you've gone away

Wayward Wind

Wayward wind, do you know your name
restless heart, can you smell the rain
Haunting songs, the desert sings
through the wires, you sweet voice rings

Shattered dreams, like desert sands
laugh along, the burning strand
Morning star, blushes 'cross the plain
evening palls, the bleeding sage

Silver stars, on velvet painted skies
the wayward wind, to tomorrow rides

Cowboy's Lament

Rolling outta Cheyenne on a Monday
pushin a thousand head of Texas grade A
too tired to stop, too cold to go on
I pull up my collar -
haven't seen the sun in four whole days

Raining too hard to cook supper
and breakfast is still a river away
the night is a sea of darkness
that swallowed the desert up whole
I pull up my collar -
haven't seen the sun in four whole days

Desert sky is pouring down hard
wastin off the brim of my hat
and my body is soaked to the bone
dried up old riverbed, black mud turning south
leading me so far from home
I pull up my collar-run my fingers through your hair
haven't seen the sun in four whole days

The River Waits

Harmonica plays a haunting tune
across the slumbering windswept plain
while lights of blues and prismic hues
laugh in the northern sky

campfires tame the bitter frost
that rides on evening's solemn shade
empty stares, and steely glares
until tomorrow—the river waits

This Old Hat

If this old hat could talk
oh the tales it would tell
of angry rogues and winter storms,
the warm embrace that said it all.

If this old hat could talk, it might tell the tales
of honky tonks and poker games
or the night the river rose
behind the early rains

If this old hat could speak
then surely it would tell
of howling winds, and the ways
tarnished laughter hides the pain
of spurs and chaps
and stuff like that
buried 'neath this cowboy's hat

But this old hat hangs quiet
from a hock upon the wall
keeping all it's secrets
nor ever letting on
here hangs the heart of a cowboy
if only, it could talk

The Desert Rose

The beauty of the desert rose
no, may not be found
in the mist of dawn's first kiss
that glistens on her lips.
Nor in her slender body, that
dances with the heartbeat
of the wind
The beauty of the desert rose
never will be found
in the pastel shaded powder
that softly dusts her blushing cheeks.
Nor be it in her sweet perfume
that whispers, on the nuance
of a summer breeze
No, the beauty of the desert rose
if nature's riddles will impart,
to know the beauty of the desert rose
you first must know her heart

Silver Belt Buckle

A silver belt buckle
and a good heart of gold
they say he's a cowboy
but he just don't know
its been so long
since he's been down that road
with his silver belt buckle
and a good heart of gold

A dusty old Stetson
and brown leather boots
he'd shoot out the stars
and rope you the moon
he don't ever say much
for his thoughts are his own
like the silver belt buckle
and good heart of gold

Time is no ally
for this rodeo man
she'd love him if he let her
but she can't understand
why he chases a dream
of so long ago
of a silver belt buckle
and a good heart of gold

I Wish I Had a Horse That Didn't Drink So Much

I wish I had a horse
That didn't drink so much
This lazy old gray mare's
Just drank down my last buck

Two dollars in my pocket
Just don't go that far
When the cattle's in and the boss's asleep
And there's the two of us at the bar

What'll it be there cowboy
The bartender knew my game
A shot and a beer there barkeep
My horse'll have the same

Y'all cain't bring no horse in here
The bartender did exhort
This here's a place of commerce
Not for swillin some dumb horse

Now I was suddenly set aback
As I pounded down my braugh
This here isn't no regular horse I said
This girl's been around

I won her in a card game
Aces fell for my bluff
Since then we bin together
But she sure does drink too much

I'll admit she ain't much to look at
And she ain't much of a ride
and I wish I had a dollar
for every achin mile
But she's bin 'n a Roy Rodgers movie
Bin on the old' Chissome trail
Spent time in the local hoosgal
And run out on a rail

Swilled beer in Kansas city
Jack Black in Arkansas
Tequila down in some ol' Mexican town
So barkeep, bring 'em on

We ain't lookin for no trouble
I smiled, beneath my Dapper Dan veneer
That's fine by me the barkeep said
But we don't serve no horses here

Now pardner if you don't mind
I stared that barkeep down
Here's my one last dollar
Fetch us up a round
Just line 'em on the counter
And just leave me to my luck
cause I wish I had a horse
That didn't drink so much

Streams in the Desert

Silent streams in the desert flow
calmly through the blister'd sand.
Laughing among the inlaid rocks
polishing and shaping stones,
with gentle insistence.

Washing 'way footprints of the past
and sculpting subtle, intended change.
With tendril arms that reach out, to touch
those strolling along the sloping banks,
who will not see.

Swollen banks that spring anew
though cleverly hidden by design.
Meander along a preset course
the essence of life in their bosom sewn,
and bearing His promises,
as though silent streams in the desert,
flow.

Lace & Whiskey Intertwined

Soft as evening, warm as spring
cool satin nights of whisper'd dreams
soft warm glow, warm red wine
lace and whiskey intertwined
velvet tones, silent moans
echo passions…of a minstrel's prose
slow music plays, blue silver light
subtle strains of sweet fire and ice
venus the muse of intricate verse while
longing fingers trace supple curves
rose petal blush of teardrops borne
soft to the touch when we're alone
Darkness smothers passion's cries
lace and whiskey intertwined

The Ghosts of Westray

Two hundred or so, so many years ago
they came from the shores of Britannia
The crags are the hosts of the cold Atlantic coast
the bottom of the world is a stranger

The keepers of night, at the breath of first light
disappear into the darkness
to leave those they love for picks, shovels and blood
when the light of the morning star beckons

Sing a song of life and love
for the sons of the Westray adventure
sing a song of life and love
for the mountain's claimed her tenure

The ninth day of May tolled the telltale bane
in a tempest forever remembered
Just before dawn the buildings were gone
as smoke columned into the stillness

Young mothers cried as the rescuers tried
to pull out what the mountain surrender'd
A row of hard-hats sits quietly in wait
of the ghosts of the Westray adventure

Can you abide the twenty six who have died
money and profit the good rules of commerce
Twenty six men never heard from again
keep dark,
wash your hands of the Westray disaster

Sing a song of life and love
for the sons of the Westray adventure
sing a song of life and love
for the mountain's claimed her tenure

Two hundred or so, so many years ago
they came from the shores of Britannia
The crags are the hosts of the cold Atlantic coast
the bottom of the world is no stranger
to the sons of the Westray adventure

These Woods

These woods are quiet now
No more the ramp of season's wrath
Clatters through the deaden lore
As echoes bide upon a stage
Of cobalt gray
Silhouettes dance on filaments
Of winter breath
The welcome silence whispers forth
To chase
Along the hollow halls
The crunch of snow the only sound
These woods are silent now

How Quietly the Desert Sleeps

How quietly the desert sleeps
Embraced in midnight-velvet sheets
As lavender clouds drift aimlessly
Across a purple melded sky
Through the night, the warm wind sings
Whispers through her violin dreams
As stars aloft on gossamer strings ebb on waning twilight tides
Dawn breaks the spell with lilac streaks
Soft kisses play upon her cheeks
Stirring life, and awakening dreams
As suncast fingers gently glide
Still…the desert so quiet lies

Winterscape

The snow is falling
I sit and watch, the flakes that fall
In silent ways blows drifts
That pitch and roll
Upon an endless sea

The snow is falling
I sit a watch, a steely blue
And painted sleigh on which
To chase the wind
Down frozen snow-clad banks

The snow is falling
I sit and watch, a steaming pot
Fogs window panes, hot soup
To chase the chill
Of a bitter winter

Windsong

The mountain sings a gentle breeze
down tree lined paths of evergreen,
in whispers kissing tender limbs
that glisten of the morning mist.
Dancing o'er the painted lea
echoes of serenity, in
windsong dreams of fragrant sighs
beneath a veil of soft moonlight.
Her argent tears a gentle rain
the mountain song a sweet refrain,
through placid vale the melody rings
a gentle breeze, the mountain sings

A December Day

December, and the silent hills
still'd with winter's breath,
a silken dusk with weather
on the horizon
as dervish specters race
through evenings waning tides.

I stood and stared
to watch, to listen
to know the voice of the darkened sky
as spruces wrought
with laden boughs
welcome seasons' angst.
I am warm
with the reflection of
the amber flame,
against the frosted pane

Dusty Gravel Roads

Legend holds the secrets
of dusty gravel roads
men who rode in silence
eyes as cold as snow
weather worn upon their faces
riding long against the wind
nights so long and lonely
when it was too darn cold

We laid ol' Happy down
on a cold and rainy day
two dollars in his pocket
we used to mark his grave
then rode off in the twilight
bleeding off our wounds
knowin' we'd be joinin' him
on that road someday

Lonely, tawdry bars, the smell
of sawdust on the floor
all that now remains
of who went on before
when hardy men of legend
sang, "that old rugged cross"
riding open prairie skies
down dusty gravel road's